CAUT
warned that this play is subject to royalty. It is fully p
Original Works Publishing, and the copyright laws of the United
States. All rights, including professional, amateur, motion
pictures, recitation, lecturing, public reading, radio broadcasting,
television, and the rights of translation into foreign languages are
strictly reserved.

The performance rights to this play are controlled by
Original Works Publishing and royalty arrangements and licenses
must be secured well in advance of presentation. No changes of
any kind shall be made to the work, including without limitation
any changes to characterization, intent, time, place, gender or race
of the character. PLEASE NOTE that amateur royalty fees are set
upon application in accordance with your producing circumstances.
When applying for a royalty quotation and license please give us
the number of performances intended, dates of production, your
seating capacity and admission fee. Royalty of the required
amount must be paid whether the play is presented for charity or
gain and whether or not admission is charged. Royalties are
payable with negotiation from Original Works Publishing.

Due authorship credit must be given anywhere the title
appears, on all programs, printing and advertising for the play. The
name of the Playwright must appear on a separate line, in which no
other name appears, immediately beneath the title and in size and
prominence of type equal to 50% of the largest, most prominent
letter used for the title of the Work. No person, firm or entity may
receive credit larger or more prominent than that accorded to the
Playwright.

Copying from this book in whole or in part is strictly
forbidden by law, and the right of performance is not transferable.
The purchase of this publication does not constitute a license to
perform the work.

Whenever the play is produced the following notice must
appear on all programs, printing, and advertising for the play on
separate line:

**"Produced by special arrangement with
Original Works Publishing.
www.originalworksonline.com"**

The Brink
© Eugenie Carabatsos
Trade Edition, 2022
ISBN 978-1-63092-132-3

Also Available From
Original Works Publishing

SMOKE AND FIRE by F.J. Hartland
Synopsis: He was bullied in elementary school… and in middle school… and in high school. Now a boy named Hilary is taking matters into his own hands to stop that bullying. Permanently. Blurring the past, the present and the future, six characters struggle with events leading up to a fateful point in time when their lives could converge in tragedy.
Cast Size: 4 Females, 2 Males

The Brink
by Eugenie Carabatsos

CHARACTERS

Helen: Early 20s, she/her, any race/ethnicity

Charlie: Early 20s, he/him, she/her, they/them, or gender nonconforming, any race/ethnicity

Josh: Early 20s, he/him, any race/ethnicity

Marcus: Early 20s, he/him, white.

SETTING
Charlie's apartment

NOTE
Characters should literally "build the memories." Furniture, props, and even people can be moved around and placed accordingly. There can be instances when furniture and props from memories remain during the present day scenes. In other words, there should be a melting of memories and reality. This should come to a head in the final "taboo" scene, where Josh and Marcus's presence should be felt, and even acknowledged, when Helen and Charlie are in the present.

Please adjust Charlie's pronouns to fit the performer.

The Brink was first produced in the Midwinter Madness Festival in New York in 2012. The production was directed by Harry Poster. The cast was as follows:

HELEN   Sabina Friedman-Seitz
CHARLIE   Andrew Wells Ryder
MARCUS   Christopher Davis
JOSH   Jonny Price

This play is dedicated to Nick.

THE BRINK

(Charlie and Helen are kissing. They break apart.)

CHARLIE: I'm sorry.

HELEN: What?

CHARLIE: I should be sorry, right?

HELEN: I'm sorry too. It's okay. This happens to friends all the time.

CHARLIE: It does?

HELEN: I don't know. Does it?

CHARLIE: Maybe. Okay, well should we just pretend this never happened?

HELEN: Should?

CHARLIE: Yes, should?

HELEN: Meaning maybe we shouldn't?

CHARLIE: You're reading into this a little too much.

HELEN: Well should or shouldn't we?

CHARLIE: I don't think it matters whether we should or shouldn't because we won't be able to.

HELEN: Yes, sure we can. Just ignore it. We know how to ignore feelings now. Don't we? Sorry, that was kind of dark wasn't it? It's just... well, you understand. Do you feel as though you've changed?

CHARLIE: Changed?

HELEN: Fundamentally.

CHARLIE: Yes.

HELEN: Me too. Sorry. I didn't mean for it to get so depressing. At least not right away. I've kept it together for a couple weeks now. Then, I see you. I see you for a minute and I just let it go.

CHARLIE: Let what go?

HELEN: The joke. I just feel comfortable being depressed around you.

CHARLIE: You're welcome.

HELEN: Only you would understand that as a compliment.

CHARLIE: But you've had happy moments in the past few months.

HELEN: Sure. Moments. And you?

CHARLIE: Getting your postcards.

HELEN: Oh, good.

CHARLIE: Yes, all of those amazing places you went.

HELEN: Right.

CHARLIE: London, Dublin, Madrid—

HELEN: Prague, Paris, yes, yes, yes.

CHARLIE: I still want to go to Europe.

HELEN: Yes, you should. How's work?

CHARLIE: Fine.

HELEN: Do you like it?

CHARLIE: No.

HELEN: Are you still applying to law school?

CHARLIE: No. Hey, do me a favor. Let's not talk about the future.

HELEN: I'm just trying to make conversation.

CHARLIE: You don't have to do that. Let's just talk.

HELEN: I couldn't really sleep when I was away.

CHARLIE: Did you drink? That usually helps me.

HELEN: But it doesn't stop me from dreaming.

CHARLIE: No that's true. I had that dream again last night.

HELEN: The dream? You have got to stop blaming yourself for what happened, Charlie. I had a new one the other night.

CHARLIE: Oh?

HELEN: I tried to scream but nothing would come out and I couldn't wake myself up, even though I knew it was a dream. I hate that. It's like you're trapped in your own mind and what's worse is—

CHARLIE: You know it.

HELEN: Exactly.

(Josh and Marcus enter and help Helen and Charlie build the scene. Helen narrates as they get set up. Once the scene is set, Marcus exits.)

HELEN: It always starts off the same way. We're sitting in Josh's living room, having a drink. We're all chatting, not about anything important. I look at the clock, it's 9:58 and I register the time. I'm not quite sure why, but I do. I'm telling you guys about my impending European vacation and even as I speak, I know something horrible is going to happen.

(Marcus enters with a gun. As Helen narrates, they act out the scene.)

HELEN: I know it is going to happen. But I can't warn you. I can't do anything. And all of a sudden, he just starts shooting. He shoots Josh three times and then he turns to you and I beg with him, plead with him not to kill you, but he does it. He kills you. And the blood just keeps rushing all around me in a pool and it encircles me and I can't keep my eyes off of it and he stares at me. He stares at me, willing the blood to drown me. And then I look up at him. I look into his eyes and he holds the gun straight at my head. Before I can say anything, before I can ever say his name, he quickly turns the gun on himself and shoots. His body collapses to the floor and I am surrounded. Surrounded by all three of you. I cannot move. I am alone. Alone and immersed in blood. Then I don't see any of you anymore. Just red. Red, as I start to drown. Just when I can't gasp from my breath anymore, I wake up.

(Josh and Marcus exit, leaving Helen and Charlie in the present day.)

CHARLIE: I'm sorry.

HELEN: You died.

CHARLIE: I'm sorry.

HELEN: You left me alone to drown.

CHARLIE: It wasn't on purpose. Have you tried sleeping pills? They help sometimes.

HELEN: Obviously not that much. You still have that dream.

CHARLIE: Yes.

(Josh enters and they start to build the scene again. Charlie narrates.)

CHARLIE: Josh and I are sitting in the living room talking when you come in. You have just finished your neuroscience final and you look exhausted, but pleased. You say something about how you conquered the brain. It's dramatic, but, for some reason, I believe you. You throw down your backpack and plop onto the couch making some kind of exclamation about your exam. Josh goes to the refrigerator and grabs you a beer. You take a sip and then look at me. You're about to say something... I can't figure out what it is but then you're interrupted by a loud banging on the door. I go to answer it and there's Marcus. Something has come over him. At first, I think he's drunk, but it is more like he's possessed. He pushes by me and staggers over to face Josh. You try to grab his hand as he walks by. He lets you, but only for a moment and not for long enough for you to say anything. He then faces Josh and takes out the gun.

"Marcus! Marcus, what are you doing? Marcus, you don't want to do that. Everything is going to be okay. You're going through a hard time, Marcus. You don't want to use that gun. But things will get better. I promise you. They will get better."

MARCUS: "You don't know that."

CHARLIE: "Yes. I do. I promise. The end of a relationship is hard. You think about it every day now, but things will get easier. They will get better. There are still good things in life. There are still things that make life worthwhile. You don't want to do this."

(The speech isn't working. Marcus points the gun firmly at Josh.)

CHARLIE: "She's not worth it!"

(A moment, then, Marcus puts the gun down.)

CHARLIE: "Good. Good job, buddy. There you go. You're doing the right thing. Everything is fine now."

HELEN: And then you wake up?

(Marcus and Josh exit.)

CHARLIE: Yes.

HELEN: At least it's not violent.

CHARLIE: It's worse.

HELEN: You can't keep blaming yourself for what happened. You couldn't have done anything. You were in shock.

CHARLIE: Still. You always want to think that you would be capable of handling a crisis. That you could come out of it—

HELEN: A hero?

CHARLIE: Well, yes.

HELEN: I understand the impulse, Charlie, but the fact is it didn't happen that way and you can't go back and talk him out of it. No matter how many dreams you have.

CHARLIE: And you can't go back in time and die too.

HELEN: I know.

CHARLIE: Is that what you wish? Do you wish he had killed you too?

HELEN: What? No. Not most of the time, anyway.

CHARLIE: Helen—

HELEN: I mean the thought has crossed my mind now and again. But only for a moment. I don't actually wish that. Of course I don't. I know there are things to live for.

CHARLIE: Like?

HELEN: My parents. My work... I want a career. My friends. You. I wouldn't want to leave you in this fucked up situation. It's dangerous here.

CHARLIE: Where?

HELEN: Reality. I wouldn't want to leave you here alone. You could go crazy. Plus, we have a buddy system thing going on.

CHARLIE: What do you mean? Are we bringing each other away from the edge or something?

HELEN: Not exactly. I picture it more like we are on opposite sides of the brink of total madness and despair, facing each other. We both lean forward, as though we are about to fall, but because we are doing it at the same time, because we are doing it together, we become stuck. We can't both fall through, you see. We hold each other there. There we are hovering over the brink, but never falling. Forever.

CHARLIE: That's oddly comforting.

HELEN: It's a good buddy system.

CHARLIE: I go over it again and again in my head. At work, at home, before I go to sleep. I can't get it out of my head.

HELEN: The event?

CHARLIE: Yes. No. The dream. What I don't understand is that it all happened so slowly. And yet, I still couldn't do anything to stop it.

HELEN: Well there is some scientific explanation for that... if you find science to be a comfort.

CHARLIE: Go on.

HELEN: Basically, you only think the event happened slowly in retrospect. Normally your memories are formed in the hippocampus, but when you are in a dangerous or intense situation the amygdala, which is like the fear center of the brain, anyway... it activates. So you are processing more information per second Your brain is going into overdrive and—

CHARLIE: What's the point?

HELEN: The point is the actual event doesn't seem to take longer when it is happening. It is only in retrospect, only in your memory, that it seems as though time has slowed down. The memory of the event is more detailed, so you think the event itself was long.

CHARLIE: Therefore?

HELEN: You shouldn't worry about it too much because it is only in retrospect that it went by slowly.

CHARLIE: Even if that is true, it doesn't help.

HELEN: No, it doesn't.

CHARLIE: Can we go over it again?

HELEN: Again?

CHARLIE: Yes.

HELEN: We've gone over it so many times. For the police, for the newspapers, for ourselves... almost every day for months.

CHARLIE: When you were gone we didn't go over it.

HELEN: You said you think about it all day every day.

CHARLIE: Yes, but we don't go over it together.

HELEN: Charlie—I don't want to go through it again.

CHARLIE: Please, Helen. The brink, remember?

HELEN: Alright.

(Josh enters and helps set up the scene. Helen exits.)

CHARLIE: 9:56. Josh and I are sitting having a few beers and you enter.

HELEN *(re-entering)*: I officially conquered the brain!

JOSH: Congrats! Have a beer!

HELEN: The brain and the greatest authors of all time! I have conquered the brain and Shakespeare and Hemingway and the freaking Waste Land! Four years and millions of pages later, I have conquered the brain and the literary canon!

(Josh hands her a beer.)

JOSH: I was just telling Charlie that he's going to hate his new job.

HELEN: You got it?

CHARLIE: It's just paralegal work. Until I go to law school.

HELEN: Well congrats! I knew you were going to get it. And yeah, you're going to hate it.

CHARLIE: Thanks for being so supportive.

HELEN: What happened to becoming a sports writer?

CHARLIE: I don't want to be a sports writer. I have loans.

JOSH: I have loans too, but I'm not going to sell my soul.

CHARLIE: Not all of us want to do the non-profit thing.

JOSH: I decided not to take that job, actually.

HELEN: What, why?

JOSH: I'm going to move to Costa Rica and teach surfing instead.

CHARLIE: $200,000 later you are moving to Costa Rica and teaching surfing?

HELEN: I think that's great.

CHARLIE *(to Josh)*: Are you serious?

JOSH: Oh calm down, it's not forever. Just a few months. My entire life all I've done is work hard to get to the next level. First it was getting into the private boarding school, then it was getting into a good college, then it was doing well in that college so that you could get that perfect job. But the thing is, I went to college, I worked hard, I'm graduating with a degree in business... and I still have no fucking idea what I want to do.

CHARLIE: So your answer is surfing?

JOSH: I like surfing.

CHARLIE: How are you going to pay off your loans teaching surfing?

JOSH: I haven't thought about it too much yet.

CHARLIE: Do you know what your interest rates are going to be?

JOSH: I imagine they are going to be bad.

CHARLIE: Yes. Bad. Very, very bad. Isn't there something else, anything else that you would want to do? Something that would... make money?

JOSH: I'm twenty-two years old. Other than my loans, I don't have any responsibilities.

CHARLIE: You have $50,000 worth of responsibilities!

JOSH: And I will pay it back! But think about it. I'm twenty-two years old and other than my $50,000 loan, I have no other responsibilities. When else is that going to happen in life? I want to do something fun.

HELEN: Good for you. That's exactly why I'm spending my summer in Europe.

JOSH: I just need a break from my life.

CHARLIE: From what happened with Meredith?

HELEN: If Josh wants to go to Costa Rica, then it's up to him!

JOSH: Are you just being supportive because you feel bad for me? Because you think I'm lost in the world and I need some time to cleanse or whatever? Because that's not why I'm going and if that's why you're supportive then I don't want your support, Helen.

HELEN: That's not what I meant.

JOSH: I've dealt with it. She got pregnant. She had an abortion. We stopped seeing each other— fucking each other. It wouldn't have been my first choice, but it happened. And everyone should stop worrying about me. If there is anyone we should be worried about, it's Marcus.

HELEN: He didn't show up for our final. I tried to call him afterwards, but I didn't get an answer.

CHARLIE: Things will be better once we graduate and he can go home. He just needs to get out of here.

JOSH: Well if he would have talked to me about it, I would have told him to take some time off.

CHARLIE: Why? So you wouldn't have to hide the fact that you were fucking his girlfriend?

HELEN: Charlie!

JOSH: Are you ever going to stop with that? You don't even like Marcus!

CHARLIE: Doesn't matter. You didn't handle that situation well.

JOSH: I am aware of that. I don't need you and your high and mighty morals up my ass about it. People get tired of hearing you tell them what they are doing wrong, you know. We're all human. We all fuck up. The only reason you're the exception is because you never put yourself out there to do anything. Do you really think you're better than me because of this?

HELEN: He has a moral reflex, Josh. You know that. He can't stop himself.

JOSH: Well it's extremely irritating.

(Knock at the door. Charlie answers.)

CHARLIE: Marcus.

HELEN: Marcus! What happened to you today? Did you forget about the final? Marcus? Marcus? Are you okay? Marcus, hey, are you okay?

JOSH: Stop looking at me like that. What are you doing here?

(Marcus pulls out his gun.)

JOSH: Holy sh—

(Helen and Charlie duck down. Josh tries to dive under the table as Marcus shoots him. Helen crawls to Josh.)

HELEN: Oh my god.

CHARLIE: Helen, what are you doing?

HELEN: Marcus. Marcus. Oh god.

(Marcus watches as Helen holds Josh. He points the gun at her.)

CHARLIE *(is he in the past or present? Both)*: Stop!

(Marcus turns the gun on himself and shoots. Blackout. In the dark, Marcus and Josh exit. Lights up on Helen and Charlie. After a moment, they come back to present.)

CHARLIE: What the hell were you thinking? You just went over to him. You got right in front of a shooter.

HELEN: I was trying to save Josh.

CHARLIE: You could have gotten yourself killed.

HELEN: I had to stop the bleeding.

CHARLIE: You could have died.

HELEN: He could have just as easily turned and shot us dead too.

CHARLIE: You can't be so reckless with your life.

HELEN: I'm not reckless with anything. And you, you could use a little recklessness in your life.

CHARLIE: Oh you think you're Josh now?

HELEN: You do everything by the book. You're not passionate about anything.

CHARLIE: That's not true.

HELEN: You're so focused on doing what you think you need to do, you miss everything.

CHARLIE: What is that supposed to mean?

HELEN: In the four years I've known you, you have never gone out on a date. Not once.

CHARLIE: I don't know how the conversation suddenly switched to my relationship issues all of a sudden. Stop preaching your nonsense to me, Helen. You act all superior when you're really just as paralyzed, just as emotionally crippled, as I am. Stop setting different rules for me than you have for yourself.

HELEN: Okay.

CHARLIE: And you shouldn't have gotten in front of Marcus.

HELEN: Okay.

CHARLIE: You could have died Helen.

HELEN: I'm sorry.

CHARLIE: And don't tell me I don't have passion. I have passion. Just because I don't find the need to broadcast my emotions to the world, doesn't mean I don't feel anything.

HELEN: I know. I'm sorry.

CHARLIE: You, of all people, should know that.

HELEN: Yes, I do. I'm sorry. You must miss him.

CHARLIE: All of the time.

HELEN: He didn't mean what he said to you, Charlie.

CHARLIE: Yes he did.

HELEN: Well, he did, but he loved you. You were his best friend. You guys couldn't be more different. When he first introduced me to you, I was kind of surprised. You weren't his usual buddy.

CHARLIE: What do you mean?

HELEN: Well he was kind of a frat boy, wasn't he? Super social. One of those guys everyone on campus knew.

CHARLIE: Thanks.

HELEN: No, I just mean that you are a lot more reserved.

CHARLIE: I'm aware.

HELEN: I'm just saying I was surprised! Don't take it as an insult. If anything, it's an insult to Josh. I didn't think he would befriend someone so serious and directed. *(Beat.)* I miss Marcus too. Sometimes.

CHARLIE: How could you miss a person like that?

HELEN: I miss how he was when we first met him. I miss the person he could have been.

CHARLIE: He was a killer, Helen. He killed his friend. He could have killed you.

HELEN: Something overcame him. He was grieving; he didn't know how to handle it.

CHARLIE: Plenty of other people grieve; they don't go out and kill people because of it.

HELEN: I know that. But he was sick, Charlie. And we didn't realize how sick he was. We were the closest to him. His family was across the country. We were the ones dealing with him on a daily basis and we had no idea what was going on.

CHARLIE: His girlfriend broke up with him. That's it. She broke up with him. Break ups can be hard, but seriously. It's just a freaking relationship. He was betrayed by Josh. I get it. Josh was his friend and he betrayed him by sleeping with his girlfriend. But that is all that happened. It's not worth killing over. I can never, ever forgive him for what he did.

HELEN: No one is talking about forgiveness, Charlie.

CHARLIE: You are—

HELEN: I'm not! I'm just saying it's more complicated that you make it out to be.

CHARLIE: No, Helen. It isn't. He killed someone. He killed an innocent person. That means he is an evil person. It doesn't get much more evil than that.

HELEN: He was a sick person, Charlie. We should have realized it. I should have realized it, in any case. I spent the most time with him. After Meredith broke up with him and he started to fall into depression, I tried to see him every day until the end of the semester. I mean, it had been months, months after the breakup and I was still trying to see him all the time. Because he was still fading and he was doing worse. He was so angry and never went to class. But then it was the end of the semester; it had been almost six months since she broke up with him. Finals were coming up and you know what? I was tired of it. Tired of hearing him talk about her. About how angry he was. About how much he missed her. Loved her. It was exhausting. And no one else was talking to him about it!

CHARLIE: Are you blaming me for this?

HELEN: I'm just asking why I was the only one who was comforting him throughout this whole thing? You knew just as well as I did that he was falling apart.

CHARLIE: Yes and that's why I stopped trying to be friends with him. He wasn't himself anymore.

HELEN: You can't just abandon people when they're down, Charlie.

CHARLIE: He was gone. He was toxic to be around.

HELEN: He was your friend. You owed him something. Your time. Your freaking shoulder to cry on.

CHARLIE: I gave him my time. I gave him a freaking shoulder to cry on. But I had to stop, because it was unhealthy and exhausting as you said. He couldn't think about anything else. He couldn't do anything else. He wasn't himself anymore.

HELEN: Is that what you're going to do to me?

CHARLIE: What?

HELEN: Are you going to stop being my friend when you think I'm going off the edge?

CHARLIE: Jesus, Helen, shut up. Stop comparing yourself to a murderer!

HELEN: I'm not comparing myself to a murderer, Charlie. He's our friend. He's Marcus!

CHARLIE: Newsflash: Marcus is a murderer!

HELEN: That isn't the only thing that defines him!

CHARLIE: It's the only thing that matters now. And don't blame me for this sense of guilt you have about Marcus. It wasn't my job to fix him and it wasn't yours either. You couldn't have stopped him. You said it yourself, he was sick.

(Beat.)

HELEN: I shouldn't have blamed you. It's not your fault my priorities shifted. They shouldn't have shifted.

CHARLIE: You were just doing what you thought was right at the time.

HELEN: I was being selfish.

CHARLIE: You can't blame yourself for him going over the edge, just like I can't blame myself for not stopping Marcus as it was happening.

HELEN: It's just so fucked up.

CHARLIE: Yes, it is.

HELEN: Just so fucked up. You think you have your own plan all laid-out and then, suddenly, you realize that someone else had a completely different plan for you. A violent plan.

CHARLIE: The loss of control is...

HELEN: Unbearable. It's like you're not in charge of your fate anymore. Remember the night after, when everyone was over here?

That's kind of how I felt then. As though other people were intruding on us. They were grieving too. I know that. And I know they just wanted to be supportive and help out, but at the time, it felt almost voyeuristic.

CHARLIE: Because they kept asking questions and asking if we were okay.

HELEN: I never realized how stupid that question was, "Are you okay?" Of course I'm not okay, I just witnessed a murder/suicide. It's almost like a reflex... something bad happens, you ask "Are you okay?" the answer is always no. No one is okay. And those that think they are okay are just fooling themselves.

CHARLIE: But we used to ask each other that question all of the time. Remember?

HELEN: Yes, but we meant it differently. It wasn't a reflex; we were asking about each other's state of mind. It wasn't a question at all. It was an assertion. "You are okay." "You are okay and I am okay and we are okay because we are together."

CHARLIE: It was weird, being so intimate.

HELEN: It made sense at the time. You were the only person I wanted to be with. Remember, *(they transition back in time)* the last person had finally left your house. You were sitting on the couch, drinking and I was basically shoving them out the door. I slammed the door, turned around and looked at you. They're gone.

CHARLIE: Finally.

HELEN: Nice of them to come.

CHARLIE: Yes.

HELEN: They were all crying. All of them.

CHARLIE: Yeah I know.

HELEN: I've never seen so many people crying at one time.

CHARLIE: Shocking news.

HELEN: They weren't even there. They weren't even there and they were crying hysterically.

CHARLIE: The idea is horrific enough.

HELEN: But no one would stop crying. It was infuriating. It was so loud.

CHARLIE: We can be quiet now.

HELEN: Yes. Finally.

(Helen goes to get a drink. She takes her time. They both enjoy the silence but are also disturbed by it.)

HELEN: Okay you need to talk to me now.

CHARLIE: What?

HELEN: I just want to be sure you're there.

CHARLIE: I'm here. You can see me.

HELEN: I just want to make sure. Josh's parents are coming tomorrow.

CHARLIE: Yeah.

HELEN: They are going to want to see us.

CHARLIE: Yeah.

HELEN: What are we going to say to them?

CHARLIE: I don't know.

HELEN: Do you think Marcus's parents will come?

CHARLIE: I don't know.

HELEN: What are we going to say to them?

CHARLIE: I don't know, Helen.

HELEN: What am I going to say to my parents?

CHARLIE: Whatever you want.

HELEN: Well what are you going to tell your dad?

CHARLIE: Nothing. I don't really talk to my dad that much.

HELEN: You're not going to tell him anything?

CHARLIE: Well I'm sure he'll read about, so it will probably come up. But I don't think it's going to be a long conversation. Probably something like, "I'm sorry. I'm glad you're safe." End of discussion.

HELEN: Not that close I guess?

CHARLIE: Not really. You're close to your parents though, right?

HELEN: Pretty close.

CHARLIE: That's good.

HELEN: Yeah. Do you think Josh and Marcus were close to their parents?

CHARLIE: Josh was.

HELEN: I think Marcus was too.

CHARLIE: Honestly, I wish he would have just killed himself. He didn't need to take someone else with him.

HELEN: I've thought that too. What does that say about us? That we wished our friend had just killed himself?

CHARLIE: It says that we think Josh didn't deserve to die, which he didn't.

HELEN: Do you think there will be a service? Was Josh religious?

CHARLIE: I don't think so.

HELEN: I hope there's a service.

CHARLIE: Why? You're not religious.

HELEN: I know but I like tradition. I like having a place to go and mourn. I feel like I'm doing something even when I can't do anything. Plus, I like seeing other people pray.

CHARLIE: Why?

HELEN: It's comforting to know that some people have faith. Makes me feel as though maybe I'm wrong.

CHARLIE: Well if there is a service, we'll go together.

HELEN: Okay.

(They transition back to the present.)

HELEN: Josh's funeral wasn't like that.

CHARLIE: No. It wasn't.

HELEN: I've only been to funerals of old people. Sick people, usually. They had lived a long life. Even though you were mourning, you could at least comfort yourself knowing that they had at least lived a long time. This wasn't lovely. It wasn't comforting. What had Josh done in his life? He had been to school; he had made friends. He didn't even get to start doing what he wanted yet.

CHARLIE: I've never been so angry before. Angry at a funeral.

HELEN: I remember. I've never seen you like that. I didn't know you could get that angry.

CHARLIE: I hadn't been. Not for a long time.

HELEN: When we got home that night—

CHARLIE: Tears. Furious tears. I hadn't cried in years. Not since I found out my mother died. I couldn't even cry at her funeral.

HELEN: It was overwhelming... to feel so much.

CHARLIE: Yes. Do you remember when I broke that bottle? You were in the living room and I was in the kitchen.

(They transition into the memory.)

CHARLIE: I was cleaning up after our nights of drinking. I dropped a bottle.

(He drops a glass bottle; it breaks. He bends down to pick it up and cuts his hand. This may happen offstage.)

CHARLIE: Fuck!

HELEN: What happened?

CHARLIE *(entering, if not onstage already)*: Cut my hand.

HELEN: Jesus you're bleeding.

CHARLIE: Yeah.

HELEN: Does it hurt? What did you cut it on?

CHARLIE: Broke a bottle. It doesn't hurt. It feels amazing.

HELEN: What do you mean it feels amazing?

CHARLIE: To bleed. To see blood. To feel it. It's a rush; my god it's a fucking drug.

HELEN: Where's the bottle?

CHARLIE: In the kitchen.

(He watches Helen go into the kitchen. Realizing what she's about to do…)

CHARLIE: Jesus, Helen, No.

HELEN: I want that feeling.

CHARLIE: No. I'm not letting you cut yourself on purpose. Put that down come on.

(Helen uses the glass to cut her hand. Blood rushes out. She feels an overwhelming moment of relief.)

HELEN: Ha! Look! I bleed.

(They move back to the present.)

CHARLIE: Feeling something other than what we were feeling was…

HELEN: Enlivening. It's one of those feelings I will remember as long as I live. The feeling of my skin break, the vision of the blood flowing, the sting, the moment of pain, and then the release. It was better than any drug. It was better than any therapy. It was momentary, but it was the closest I had been to relief.

(Charlie looks to her. She feels his eyes and breaks out of it.)

HELEN: Everything I ever felt before the event feels so small now.

CHARLIE: And everything after…

HELEN: Right.

CHARLIE: Work, homework, school…

HELEN: And you would get so stressed out about homework. Do you remember that time you came home from the library and I was watching TV? I thought you were going to scream at me for interrupting your work environment.

CHARLIE: That wasn't it at all. I was just surprised.

HELEN: And cranky.

CHARLIE: Well it was the World Series and I was stuck in the library.

(They transition back in time. Helen sits on his couch, wearing a Yankees cap. Charlie enters.)

CHARLIE: Hey. What are you doing here?

HELEN: World Series.

CHARLIE: Don't you have a TV?

HELEN: Yours is bigger.

CHARLIE: Well I have work.

HELEN: It's almost over. Anyway, I thought maybe you'd want to watch it.

CHARLIE: I hate the Yankees.

HELEN: But it's the World Series.

CHARLIE: Why don't you watch it at Stephen's?

HELEN: He's annoying me.

CHARLIE: He's your boyfriend.

HELEN: That's why he's annoying. Come on, sit with me. Watch it.

(Charlies sits. They watch. It's the very end of the game. We hear the sounds of the Yankees winning. Charlie isn't able to handle it so he gets up and goes into the kitchen. Helen jumps around, clearly celebrating. Charlie pretends to be disgusted and disappointed, but then looks to Helen as she dances around and smiles fondly. Helen spots him watching her.)

HELEN: What? Why are you looking at me like that?

CHARLIE *(switching off the TV)*: Alright, alright, it's over.

(They face each other.)

CHARLIE: Happy?

HELEN: Yes!

CHARLIE: Good.

(They hold a gaze for a beat. Helen breaks it.)

HELEN: And that's when Marcus came in.

CHARLIE: Right.

(Back into the past. Marcus enters and disrupts the moment. He is distraught, angry.)

CHARLIE: Marcus!

HELEN: Hey. Are you okay?

MARCUS: Meredith broke up with me.

HELEN: What?

CHARLIE: I'm sorry.

HELEN: What happened?

CHARLIE: Do you want a drink?

MARCUS: Everything was going fine. And then today she just tells me she can't take me anymore.

HELEN: I'm sorry, Marcus. Break ups are hard.

CHARLIE: She would know. She breaks up with guys all of the time.

HELEN *(ignoring him)*: Can I do anything?

MARCUS: I just didn't see it coming. I just did not see it coming at all.

HELEN: I know it's hard now, but in time, you'll get over it.

MARCUS: She's the one. I was going to marry her.

CHARLIE: Seriously?

MARCUS *(to Helen)*: There's another guy, isn't there?

HELEN: Did she say that?

MARCUS: There is. I know there is. Helen, do you know the other guy?

HELEN: What? No.

MARCUS: You know something don't you?

HELEN: What? No! I wasn't friends with Meredith.

MARCUS: But she liked you. She would talk to you about things.

HELEN: I've never hung out with her outside of spending time with you. I promise you, I don't know anything. If I did, I would tell you.

MARCUS: How do I know that for sure?

HELEN: Know what?

MARCUS: That you wouldn't be protecting her!

HELEN: Because you're my friend!

MARCUS: I think you know something. You know something. Don't you?

HELEN: Marcus! Calm down! I don't know anything. Stop being an asshole. *(to Charlie)* He was really aggressive.

CHARLIE: I don't remember this at all.

HELEN: No because you weren't there. You were with Josh.

CHARLIE: That's right. Josh was there.

HELEN: Yeah he let me into your apartment.

CHARLIE: Right. I forgot. I gave him a key so he could pick up a book or something that he needed to borrow. This is what happened—

(They reset.)

CHARLIE: Marcus came in. We had that exchange.

MARCUS: I thought she was the one. I thought I was going to marry her.

(Josh enters.)

CHARLIE: Seriously?

JOSH *(to Charlie)*: Hey can I talk to you for a minute?

(Charlie and Josh move away from Helen and Marcus. As Josh and Charlie speak, Marcus may be frozen. Helen exists in present day watching the memory.)

CHARLIE: What's up?

JOSH: I need to tell you something.

CHARLIE: Dude, Marcus is really upset.

JOSH: I know.

CHARLIE: Meredith broke up with him.

JOSH: I know.

CHARLIE: Wait. How did you—

MARCUS: You know something!

CHARLIE: What the—?

(Josh and Charlie return to Helen and Marcus.)

HELEN: I promise, Marcus. I would have told you.

MARCUS: Okay. Okay.

CHARLIE: Everything okay?

HELEN: Yes. Everything's fine.

CHARLIE: Marcus, you okay, buddy?

MARCUS: Yes. I'm going home.

HELEN: I'll come with you.

(Helen and Marcus exit. After a moment, Helen re-enters in present. Josh stays.)

HELEN: And that was it.

CHARLIE: You left with him? After he was that aggressive with you?

HELEN: I had it under control.

CHARLIE: What were you thinking? He could have hurt you. He might have if we weren't there.

HELEN: Oh don't flatter yourself, Charlie. He didn't want to hurt me. There's proof of that now, isn't there? Now, what happened after we left?

CHARLIE: I don't know. Why is that important?

HELEN: Did you talk about Marcus?

CHARLIE: Maybe. Yeah. It wasn't that important whatever it was.

HELEN: I think it may have been. Can you remember? Try to remember.

CHARLIE: Okay. Well, you guys left and then it was just me and Josh.

(Transition to memory. Helen watches.)

CHARLIE: Jesus. That was a bit intense.

JOSH: He's just mad.

CHARLIE: Yeah. I never thought she'd actually dump him.

JOSH: She put up with his crap for a long time.

CHARLIE: Yeah, but still. He seems pretty convinced there was another guy. Do you think there was?

JOSH: I don't know, maybe.

CHARLIE: Helen always said that people won't break up with their current partner until they find someone else. It's an emotional insurance policy.

JOSH: Then maybe.

CHARLIE: That idea is really fucked up though, isn't it? We'd rather be with someone we don't love than be alone.

JOSH: Yeah—

CHARLIE: But what kind of guy would go after someone who has a girlfriend?

JOSH: A lot of guys.

CHARLIE: But that doesn't make it right.

JOSH: Then how would people ever get out of relationships?

CHARLIE: What?

JOSH: Based on that theory. How would people ever get out of relationships if there wasn't someone to remind the person that there are other people out there.

CHARLIE: That isn't how it works. You don't have to go after the person for that person to realize there are other people out there. It's about the feeling.

JOSH: Well some people need more than a feeling—

CHARLIE: What are you talking about?

JOSH: Nevermind.

CHARLIE: Anyway, what was it that you wanted to tell me?

JOSH: Huh?

CHARLIE: Didn't you have something to tell me?

JOSH: Oh, it's not important.

CHARLIE: Did you get what you needed?

JOSH: What?

CHARLIE: The notes or the book—

JOSH: Yeah. Thanks.

CHARLIE: Sure. So Helen came looking for me?

JOSH: She wanted to watch the game. I figured you wouldn't mind.

CHARLIE: No, of course not.

JOSH: Who won?

CHARLIE: What?

JOSH: The game?

CHARLIE: Yankees.

JOSH: Oh man that must kill you.

CHARLIE: They're not so bad.

(End of the memory. Josh exits. Charlie waits for a moment, faces Helen.)

HELEN: He was trying to tell you, Charlie. He was trying to tell you he was the guy.

CHARLIE: No he wasn't. Was he?

HELEN: Obviously. What else would it have been?

CHARLIE: Well, why didn't he tell me then?

HELEN: Because you basically told him he was a bad person.

CHARLIE: I thought they were just hooking up.

HELEN: No. Josh was the guy. Josh and Meredith were in love. It wasn't just a random hook up at the end of the year.

CHARLIE: It's easy to piece together things in retrospect. To see all of the connections—

HELEN: —Do you remember when we first met?

CHARLIE: Of course.

HELEN: That was the night that Marcus told us about Meredith.

CHARLIE: Oh. Right.

HELEN: Marcus and I were in his apartment.

(Helen sets up the scene. Marcus enters. He and Helen play "Taboo" and drink. Charlie watches in the memory.)

HELEN: We were waiting for Josh.

MARCUS: Remind me again why we are playing a board game?

HELEN: Because all we do is sit around and drink.

MARCUS: It's the weekend. That's what we are supposed to do.

HELEN: Well it'll be more interesting if there is a game involved.

MARCUS: Taboo is not a drinking game.

HELEN: Any game can be a drinking game.

MARCUS: I don't know how to play.

HELEN: It's easy—you break up into partners and—

MARCUS: —Helen, I met someone.

HELEN: Oh, that's great! Who is she?

MARCUS: Meredith. Meredith Keller.

HELEN: Oh yeah, Josh has a class with her. He was telling me about her. She sounds cool.

MARCUS: She's amazing. She's beautiful, smart, funny.

HELEN: Sounds great, Marcus.

MARCUS: I'm in love with her.

HELEN: Woah.

MARCUS: I am.

HELEN: Don't you think it may be a little early to be using you know... the "l" word.

MARCUS: No.

HELEN: How long have you two known each other?

MARCUS: Only a week or so, but I know. I know I love her. You know how I've always had that pent up aggression. Well, I have. I've been trying to hide it as best as I can since I came to college, but it's there. I just feel how can I describe it? Sometimes I just feel like I need to react. React to everything.

HELEN: I noticed you had a tendency to... blow things out of proportion.

MARCUS: I've always been this way but, Meredith, Meredith just makes me so happy. She gives me this sense of release. Like I have nothing to be angry about, ever.

HELEN: Don't you think you're putting a lot of pressure on one person?

MARCUS: No. She loves to hear this stuff.

HELEN: You've told her this?

MARCUS: Of course! She eats it up. She thinks she is my guardian angel or something.

HELEN: Marcus... This doesn't sound healthy.

MARCUS: Jesus Helen! You're such a downer all of the time.

HELEN *(jokingly gesturing to her lame board game)*: Well that's just not true.

MARCUS: It is true. You're just jealous because you don't love your boyfriend.

HELEN: I do. I think. Maybe. The point is, relationships take time.

MARCUS: Maybe for people like you. But not for me and not for Meredith. We feel intensely all of the time.

HELEN: Don't you think that may be part of your anger problem?

MARCUS: I don't have an anger problem, Helen. I'm just passionate. I just feel more than most people. But not Meredith. I told you this because I thought you'd be happy for me.

HELEN: I am happy for you.

MARCUS: No you're not. You're not happy for me. You haven't said anything to indicate that you are happy for me. You know what? I bet you're just jealous.

HELEN: What? No, that's not it.

MARCUS: Yes, yes, I bet that is what it is! You're just jealous because you think we won't be as close.

HELEN: No, I'm not worried about that.

MARCUS: Well you shouldn't be. Meredith knows that she is the one for me and no one would stand in the way of that.

HELEN: I'm not worried about that.

MARCUS: It's okay, Helen. It's okay to be jealous of your friends. I just want you to know that our relationship means a lot to me and I would never neglect it even though I found someone else.

(She gives up trying to explain.)

HELEN: Thanks.

MARCUS: So... now that that's all settled—

HELEN: What?

MARCUS: Say you're happy for me.

HELEN: You know I'm happy that you feel in love.

MARCUS: Helen—

HELEN: Fine! I'm happy that you are in love.

MARCUS: Thank you.

(Josh enters, pulls Charlie into the past.)

MARCUS: So how do we play?

JOSH: Hey! So this is Charlie. The person I was telling you about.

HELEN: Nice to meet you, Charlie. I'm Helen.

CHARLIE: Hi.

MARCUS: Marcus.

JOSH *(to Charlie)*: Want a beer?

CHARLIE: Sure thanks.

JOSH: What are you guys up to?

MARCUS: Helen was just teaching me how to play this stupid game.

JOSH: She's still on about that? Helen, how many times do I have to tell you, you don't have to justify drinking!

HELEN: I'm not trying to justify anything. I just get bored sitting here with you guys as you play video games all night.

JOSH: Not all night. Just until we're drunk enough to go out. So this is what I'm thinking... we hang out here for a bit... play a round of... what is this? Taboo? Okay. Anyway. We play a round of this game then we head out to the frats.

HELEN: Again? We always go to the frats.

MARCUS: That's because Josh is a bro now.

JOSH: What can I say? I need a healthy balance between hanging out with you two and having fun.

HELEN: We are fun. Aren't we, Marcus?

MARCUS: Not really. No.

HELEN *(to Charlie)*: So you and Josh have a class together?

(As Charlie and Helen talk, Marcus and Josh listen in, silently joking with each other about Helen and Charlie's awkward meet-cute. We get the sense that Josh and Marcus are good friends.)

CHARLIE: Yeah.

HELEN: Which one?

CHARLIE: Intro to International Relations.

HELEN: I was thinking about taking that class. Do you suggest it?

CHARLIE: Um yeah it's good.

HELEN: Well maybe next semester then. So does that mean you want to go into politics or law or something?

CHARLIE: Maybe. I don't know. Maybe I'll be a sports writer.

HELEN: That's awesome! You should do that.

CHARLIE: I was joking.

HELEN: Half.

CHARLIE: What?

HELEN: You were half-joking.

CHARLIE: Maybe. What about you?

HELEN: Neuroscience and literature.

CHARLIE: That's unusual.

JOSH: Yes, yes, Helen's a real contradiction. Anyway, let's get going. No more talking about classes. Drinking only please!

HELEN: Game time.

MARCUS: Before we get started, I have an announcement.

JOSH: Go for it.

MARCUS: I'm in love.

JOSH: Sweet.

HELEN: Don't you think that was a little impulsive of him, Josh?

JOSH: I mean, yeah, but whatever. It's love.

HELEN: Marcus, why don't you tell Josh when you met your love?

MARCUS: Monday.

HELEN: Monday. Of this week.

JOSH: Cool.

HELEN: You don't think five days is rushing things a bit?

JOSH: It's his business.

MARCUS: Thank you!

JOSH: I'm happy for you man.

MARCUS: See, this is the kind of reaction I was looking for. Thanks buddy.

JOSH: Of course. Don't listen to Helen. She needs to analyze every single event in her life.

HELEN: That's not true.

JOSH: So, who's the lucky lady?

MARCUS: I think you know her. Meredith Keller.

JOSH: I know her.

MARCUS: She's amazing.

JOSH: Yeah. So. Let's play.

(Josh and Marcus sit down. The game between Josh and Marcus continues throughout the following. When appropriate, Helen and Charlie should acknowledge Josh and Marcus, and Josh and Marcus can also watch and acknowledge Helen and Charlie. Past and present exist simultaneously in these last beats.)

CHARLIE: What's the point of this?

HELEN *(not wanting to leave the past)*: What?

CHARLIE: The point of this memory? Just to prove to ourselves that we missed something again?

HELEN: Not you. You didn't even know them yet. I missed something.

CHARLIE: Why? Why do you do this to yourself?

HELEN: The same reason you keep having that dream over and over again.

CHARLIE: But Helen, the connections, we can't use them now. We can't do anything with the information other than hurt ourselves.

HELEN: I'm not trying to hurt you. Don't you get it? This isn't your fault. This is my fault. You didn't even know them!

CHARLIE: Stop making this about you.

HELEN: I'm not making this about me. This is about what happened.

CHARLIE: We are partners! The brink, remember? We have to both lean forward at the same time so that we don't fall through. You want to push yourself over! What's wrong with you?

HELEN: I need to be reminded!

(An interruption by Marcus and Josh.)

CHARLIE: Of what? The fact that we didn't die? The fact that our friends did?

HELEN: Yes.

CHARLIE: Why?

HELEN: Because things are starting to get easier!

(Silence from everyone.)

CHARLIE: Good. That's healthy.

HELEN: Yes, I know it's healthy, but isn't it also wrong? I can't feel for people anymore. I can't feel that intensity that I did after the shooting.

CHARLIE: No one could handle that emotional intensity. You couldn't sustain a life that way.

HELEN: But that's what got me thinking, Charlie. Up until that point, I had never felt anything intensely. I never felt horror, disgust, loss, love, nothing, until that point. It was unbearable, unthinkable, but I was feeling. I was feeling all the time. And now, I don't feel anything. Is it worse to feel everything or nothing?

CHARLIE: Everything.   HELEN: Nothing.

CHARLIE: You couldn't survive if you felt everything that happens to you. Think about what you said about memory. Imagine if you lived every moment as though it were a trauma. We couldn't process things that way.

HELEN: Yes, but we would be aware. Aware of everything that was going on.

CHARLIE: There's no point to that. We wouldn't be able to do anything with the information.

HELEN: We would be able to feel.

CHARLIE: Why do you want to feel all of those things?

HELEN: Because they are real.

(Charlie grabs her hand. Neither Charlie nor Helen acknowledge the others now, but Josh and Marcus watch what happens and respond.)

CHARLIE: This is real too. The feeling of my hand wrapping around yours is real. That comfort is real. Your hands are always cold. That's real too. I warm your hands and you cool mine. Temperature is real. The intensity of emotion does not have to indicate reality.

HELEN: We kissed, Charlie.

CHARLIE *(drops her hand)*: Yes.

HELEN: Why did it happen?

CHARLIE: It just did.

HELEN: How do you feel about it?

CHARLIE: It probably happened because we haven't seen each other in a long time.

HELEN: We've never kissed before.

CHARLIE: I thought we agreed to just drop this topic. It was a mistake. We are dealing with life and death here, Helen; kissing doesn't mean much compared to that.

HELEN: Okay. *(Beat.)* When does kissing get to be important again?

CHARLIE: What?

HELEN: When are we allowed to care about things like kissing again? Like kissing and love and romance and all of that. When does that get to matter?

CHARLIE: I don't know, Helen. Whenever you want it to.

HELEN: What happens when it gets better?

CHARLIE: What?

HELEN: What happens to us when it gets better?

CHARLIE: What do you mean?

HELEN: They say it gets easier to deal with as time goes on. It's happening already. Slowly, but it is happening. I can read the news again. What happens to us when it gets better? Do we lose this?

CHARLIE: I don't know.

HELEN: All I've wanted these past few months is to be normal. To not feel this way. But Jesus, Charlie, I'm fucking terrified of normal.

CHARLIE: Me too.

HELEN: We can do sad, Charlie. We can do sad, tragic, horrific.

CHARLIE: I know. The brink.

HELEN: I want to do happy.

(Marcus and Josh smile.)

CHARLIE: Okay.

HELEN: I want to do happy with you.

CHARLIE: Okay.

HELEN: Here we are again, hovering over the brink.

(During the last line, MARCUS and JOSH face each other one last time.)

CHARLIE *(content)*: Yes, here we are.

> END OF PLAY.

*More One Acts From
Original Works Publishing*

THE DIPLOMATS by Nelson Diaz-Marcano
Synopsis: A few days before election night 2016, close friends Annie and Carlos are reunited in her small Astoria apartment during his first visit to New York since he moved to be with his husband in Florida. At first, it seems their relationship hasn't changed. That is until Carlos brings an unexpected guest; Annie's old best and estranged friend Gary. Throughout the course of the night they learn that while they may not have changed much as people, society has. Now they have to confront each other in a whole new reality and their relationships may never be the same.
Cast Size: 2 Males, 1 Female

*WINNER—2017 Fresh Fruit Festival
Outstanding Play*

RULES FOR COMING OUT WHEN YOU'RE IN THE DRIVER'S SEAT OF YOUR MOM'S CAMRY

by Jessica Marie Fisher

Synopsis: "Rules For Coming Out..." is the coming out story for people who are tired of unnecessarily dramatic and unrealistic coming out stories. Almost nobody "KNOWS" completely what their sexuality is – most people have to find the answers through trial and error. Lauren and Liam navigate love, sex, family, identity, relationship abuse and the sticky in-between of queer adolescence, while working through their own imperfect friendship.

Cast Size: 1 Female, 1 Male

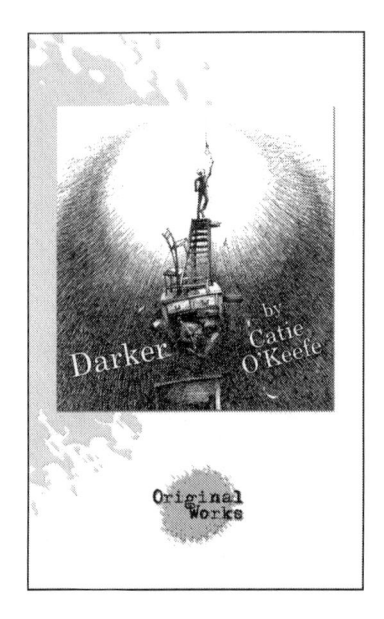

DARKER by Catie O'Keefe

Synopsis: In search of a job, Max finds himself the new kid at the Industri-Light Bulb Factory. But his surroundings are all too familiar... and he's certain he has seen his boss somewhere before. Is he losing his mind, or is this the start of a very sick- and ultimately deadly- game? Max must uncover the truth, or accept a fate that will keep his life in a mind-numbing limbo.

Cast Size: 2 Males, 1 Female

NOTES

NOTES

Made in the USA
Columbia, SC
18 May 2022